Radical Hiring Success

*Headhunter Secrets To Target Top Talent
From Your Competitors*

By Mike Adamo

Radical Hiring Success:

*Headhunter Secrets To Target Top Talent
From Your Competitors*

ISBN: 978-0-9981006-2-3

Also by Mike Adamo:
*This Book Will Get You Hired For The Job You
Want* (2016)

This book is dedicated to Tori, Natalie, Blake and Luci.

Without your support, love and patience I would never be able to get up at 4:00 AM every day to write this book.

Table of Contents

Introduction

Are you struggling to make good hires or fill a current opening? Or maybe you've had a bad hire and now you're feeling burned. You are not alone. Many people struggle with hiring. Whether you're a CEO, VP. or a new manager, the reality is: Attracting and hiring good people is difficult.

People often rise through the corporate ranks without having to recruit very many people. They rely on others to manage their hiring process, depending on associates or friends to fill vacancies or provide referrals. All those methods work, but it's the ability to identify, attract, and ultimately onboard and guide someone that you've never met, for a job you've never hired that separates out the truly successful leaders from those just skipping along through the corporate world.

In this book, I'm going to unlock the strategies I've learned as a headhunter, strategies I've honed through my two decades in recruiting. Strategies that have made me one of the best recruiters in the entire United States, able to identify and attract, and ultimately close the deal with individuals at all levels.

The key to success is understanding that all candidates want and need the same things, and are attracted by the four strategies that I'm going to lay out for you in this book.

Before we get into all that, I want to share a little bit about my background. I've been in the recruitment business for almost twenty years, ever since I graduated from college. I didn't start out wanting to be a recruiter however. Most people don't. I started out by studying exercise science at James Madison University in Virginia and getting my master's degree in exercise physiology. I thought I wanted to be a doctor, but time spent interning in hospitals during graduate school made me realize how unhappy, overworked, and underpaid physicians were. Many told me confidentially that they felt very unfulfilled. They had spent most of their early life in school trapped studying, postponing family fun, and, quite frankly, their life.

That wasn't what I wanted to do. So, after graduate school I went for a long walk. I hiked from Georgia to Maine. I didn't do this on the streets or roadways. I did this on the Appalachian Trail that runs from Springer Mountain, Georgia, to Mount Katahdin in Maine. It took me and two college buddies 103 days to make the journey on foot. Along the way, we raised money for the American Cancer Society. Steve, my hiking partner, had had cancer when he was young, and we wanted to show people that there was life after cancer.

After finishing the Appalachian Trail, I knew I wasn't going to be a professional backpacker. With a degree in exercise physiology and seven years of school under my belt, I had no idea what I was going to do. Since my uncle and cousin were in pharmaceutical sales, I decided to give it a try, believing I would be successful and make money, which was my primary goal. After interviewing for dozens of pharmaceutical jobs, I realized that I needed to gain some sales experience to get in the door.

During that process, I was approached by a recruiting firm. I had applied for a pharmaceutical sales position and they called me back for a recruiting position. I had never thought about becoming a recruiter and I had no interest in the job, but the man on the other end of the phone described to me a magical career that required no travel, yielded high income, and provided "intellectually stimulating" work. I was hooked. I was recruited into this industry by a very talented salesman. Cheers to you Bob!

What I discovered from the beginning is that recruiting people is difficult. But because I learned the secrets in this business from some very successful recruiters who'd been in it since the late 1970s at one of the most successful offices of Management Recruiters International, I became very successful. These secrets have withstood the test of time but in the digital information age have unfortunately been replaced by high volume, low quality information that managers feel compelled to sort through in their attempt to find the gems. The truth is that although technologies have changed from fax machines and phone calls to LinkedIn and emails, the successful strategies have remained the same.

Either you have dozens of junk candidates or junk information about what's going on in the market, or you have your finger on the right people and the critical information that will help your organization succeed and stay competitive. I'm going to give you a very simple strategy that involves getting rid of key behaviors that you're likely doing now and focusing instead on four secrets that will literally change the way you recruit. From how you plan, to how you target, to how you attract, and ultimately land those top performers.

I've hired thousands of people. The managers that I've worked with have ranged from CEOs and heads of HR to new managers hiring their first position. My diverse career in the recruitment industry includes almost eight years as a recruiting consultant, better known as an executive recruiter or headhunter to hundreds of companies. I've also invested over 10 years of my career working inside one of the fastest growing companies in the United States. I worked directly within Human Resources as a corporate recruiter, manager, and ultimately director of recruitment. During this time, I managed over 20 different recruiters who hired for a broad range of functions, including IT, Marketing, Accounting, Research & Development and Manufacturing. Leading recruitment assignments took me to China, Singapore, Europe, Latin America, and across the United States. I've had an opportunity to hire new college graduates, manufacturing/production workers. and business executives at all levels. I currently own a recruiting firm and hire my own staff.

This is not to brag or bore you with my background and accomplishments, but to give you a context for the advice that I will impart in the upcoming pages.

CHAPTER 1:

Get Your Foot Off the Brake Pedal, Accelerate Your Hiring

The four strategies will only work if you stop making some basic mistakes. These mistakes, or as I like to call them hiring excuses, are common to almost every person who has ever had the responsibility for hiring.

The assumptions and behaviors associated with these excuses are like a brake pedal for your hiring process. Just as the four secrets will accelerate, develop, and support your hiring success, the five excuses will derail, slow, and impede your progress. Don't step on the brakes while you attempt to depress the accelerator. Take your foot off the brake pedal and accelerate your hiring.

The Five Excuses:

Blame Others

"HR is not doing enough to help"

That statement may very well be true. Certainly, I have seen more than my share of overworked and sometimes incompetent HR folks. With tight budgets, the best HR people are overworked, often supporting very large numbers of employees and managers. They simply don't have the time to dedicate to one issue or opportunity. In smaller companies, you may not even have HR so the burden falls on you, but at least you can't blame them.

Luckily, I have a solution for you. Human Resources isn't responsible for hiring for this position. You are. You need to take ownership for getting the result your company is paying you to achieve. Over the years, I have seen too many leaders get way too focused on what HR is or is not doing to work on hiring for a position. At the end of the day, it's your responsibility to fill your open job for your company, sanity, team, and career.

Apart from the mechanics of posting a job and processing an offer, there is very little HR needs to do for you to fill your job. **Ultimately you alone must take responsibility for hiring great talent.** This mindset of ownership will change your results.

Lack of Availability

"I am too busy to interview"

This excuse reflects the common chicken or egg dilemma. Hiring people takes time. Of course, we typically don't hire someone if we are fully staffed and able to meet the demands of our role. Companies wait until their employees cry uncle to add staff. The trend is to do more with less, so we find ourselves working long hours and having more to do then we have time to accomplish. If you're a small business person you face the same issue. Fall victim to this excuse and you will never succeed at hiring or as a leader. A critical function of leadership is to secure the resources you and your team need.

The higher up you go in an organization the more demands on your time. The best leaders know how to prioritize and protect time for critical tasks that need to get done. I have worked with leaders at very high levels who flaked out on recruitment status update calls, missed interviews, and took weeks to get back to me on resumes. How quickly do you think they filled their job? Did you ever stop to consider how the quality of their candidates may have been impacted? If you don't prioritize interviewing, the good candidates will get a job before you can hire them and you will be left selecting between what remains.

Contrast the approach mentioned above with that of one of the most effective hiring leaders I ever worked with. This gentleman was running a billion-dollar business with over two thousand employees. Each week, he made it a priority to meet with me at 7:30 a.m. to review candidates, make decisions and schedule interviews. He never missed an interview or rescheduled a meeting. No matter where in the world he traveled, he made it work. Guess what? He hired better people faster. Regardless of your level or responsibility in an organization, prioritization and organization will allow you to execute tasks like hiring that are truly important.

You must make consistent investments to move your hiring process forward.

The Need to Compare

"I have not seen enough candidates"

This might be the oldest excuse in the book. Depending on how many people you need to hire, this complaint could be true. For example, maybe you have five openings and only three candidates. But if you only need to hire one position, you only need to see one person. That's right, filling your job takes one person. The trick is finding and attracting that one person and getting them to say yes.

A Hiring Lesson from a Military Sniper

I am obsessed with learning and trying new things. I once spent a weekend taking lessons from a US Marine Corps Scout Sniper. I love the Marines; my dad was a World War II marine who fought in the Pacific. Scout Snipers are the best snipers in the world; the Navy Seals developed their Sniper training program from the USMC program. The lesson here is that being a sniper is mostly boring. They learn to shoot with precise accuracy, they practice identifying and stalking their prey. Occasionally, they get an opportunity to take a real shot. And they don't miss.

The take away here is that hiring great people isn't about interviewing lots of people. It's about identifying your target, finding the right one, and getting the hire. It's not that complicated. One interview one hire. In case you're wondering yes, he did teach me to hit a thirty-six-inch disk at one thousand yards. That's ten football fields away! **You just need to find one great candidate and hire him.**

Being Overly Focused on Why People Are Not Right for Your Job / Obsessing over Requirements

"I just can't seem to find the right candidate"

This is one of the hardest excuses to change. Maybe you have a tangible candidate identification issue, but many times I hear this from leaders who have interviewed ten or more people. I know an HR Director who was hiring for a Manager level HR person who just couldn't find the right person. The position was open for six months and she had interviewed twelve people. By the time I got involved, the candidates she had interviewed early on had been hired by other companies and one even started working at the same company for a different manager. She insisted that none of these people were right. Did you ever have a single friend who was still single after many years of dating but constantly complained that there "were no good men left"?

Hiring success is about finding the critical things that you need and identifying the positive aspects of candidates. Avoid focusing on reasons not to hire people, instead focus on their positive traits. **At some point all great hiring managers make compromises. It's about finding the right balance and making a decision. Stop finding reasons not to hire anyone.**

Not Accepting the Realties of the Employment Market

"We can't pay enough to get the right people"

Sometimes you need to play the hand you're dealt. All too frequently leaders have "champagne tastes on a beer budget." The reality is that most people cannot afford many of the things that they want. Too quickly we ignore our own motivations and assume candidates don't think like us. How many of you would take a new job for less money?

The key here is to focus on what you can afford and be realistic about the profile you go after. Many great leaders have ended up hiring much younger and less experienced talent because they were going for value. Avoid the temptation to keep looking for the one person who has the experience but is much "less expensive" than the other candidates. Get more budget or hire someone with a bit less experience. Holding out to find the one underpaid person creates a high likelihood of a bad hire. While there certainly are some underpaid people that are good at what they do, the probability is that many of these folks will be poor performers. The ones who are good will likely recognize that they are underpaid and expect you to get them to market. **Align your profile and expectations with your budget and you will have a much better likelihood of making a good hire.**

Let's Review

Sometimes getting better at something is more about letting go of the bad habits that keep you from excelling. In this chapter we covered the five most common mistakes that leaders around the world at every level make every day in the hiring process. Now that you know you're not alone, stop falling victim to these mistakes and start practicing the five behaviors of hiring success:

- Assume accountability
- Prioritize hiring and put in regular consistent effort.
- Focus on finding the one right candidate.
- Stop finding reasons not to hire people.
- Align your profile and expectations with your budget.

CHAPTER 2:

Create a Focused Strategy that Targets Top Performers

Creating radical hiring success comes from clearly defining the problem you need to solve with your hire and developing a realistic market-based plan. In this chapter, we will discuss the importance of planning, how to plan, and the strategies to make your opening more attractive to top performing individuals. You'll also learn two critical talent strategies that will radically improve the probability that you will hire a top performer. Planning is the first and most critical step to consistently identify and hire top performing employees. It's also the most overlooked and poorly executed component of the hiring process. The impact of not planning is that it increases your risk of having your job open longer as well as the possibility of a bad hire. Figuring it out along the way, "hiring by trial and error," is a big mistake. During your search, your plan will naturally change and evolve, but trial and error is never an effective method of hiring.

Why Planning is Critical

I am not sure exactly why people overlook, omit or short-cut the planning phase of recruiting. It's likely a result of two causes. First, many people oversimplify or take short-cuts and assume an old job description is just fine to start with. Second, I believe many people give up on planning or become apathetic to the process because they assume it's out of their control. That's because the hiring process deals with people, and as we all know, people are very hard to predict. Many folks adopt a "let's see what we find" approach to planning due to this lack of predictability. Regardless of how unpredictable the process can be, it's critical to develop an accurate profile of the person you want to hire.

Too often execs jump right into the hiring process without considering a few critical questions. Instead, view this step as an opportunity to gather input from key stakeholders and the market, as well as to think through your own requirements. Don't be tempted to put together a boiler plate job description so you can start recruiting right away. Planning your hire *is* recruiting. If you just jump in and don't invest time on this task you will build your recruitment strategy on a weak foundation. This weak foundation will likely crumble over time, like a skyscraper erected on a base formed too quickly without adequate engineering support. Take the time to plan and build your team on a strong foundation that will last for years.

Without Establishing Your Destination, How Will You Know You Have Arrived?

A great analogy for this is sailing. Sometimes, after a long week of dealing with unpredictable people, I like to go out for a sail on my boat *Headhunter*. While I have yet to sail around the world or discover a new continent, I have cruised to Catalina Island, which is 40 miles offshore from Southern California. When I lived in New York I circumnavigated Long Island. I've cruised down the coast of California from Santa Barbara to Los Angeles. The reality of sailing is that you can't control the winds and the tides, or the weather.

If it's windy, you need to adjust your sails. If the tide's going against you, and the waves are big, and you get pushed off out to sea, you need to adjust. Sailing is a series of constant adjustments to get to where you want to go. However, you must have a final location in mind to guide the adjustments so you will arrive at your desired destination. Otherwise, you end up directionless and floating in a deep blue sea. I have seen many managers floating in a sea of resumes. If you don't identify your end goal, then you're never going to get there.

Components of an Effective Hiring Plan

Recruiting great talent is no different than any other venture. For those of us who have run large projects, we can appreciate the importance of the planning phase of any undertaking. An effective planning process maps out the deliverables of your project, the major steps, the timeline and many other items. A solid plan for recruiting top talent can simplify this process. There are three critical planning items for hiring: the candidate profile, selling the job, and identifying the candidate.

- **Develop your profile - Define your talent gap**
  - **Scope your role:** What will the person do? skills and experience; personality traits needed
  - **Validate your profile:** Get input from HR; management and market data
- **Develop your sales pitch:** Why would anyone want this job?
  - **Develop your support material**
    - Job Description
    - Critical Skills profile and candidate messaging
- **Identify how you will attract candidates**

Before we get in to the nuts and bolts of building our plan let's first establish a baseline understanding of our target.

The Case for Focusing on High Performing Individuals

Hiring great people is one of the most important things you can do as a leader. Here are a few reasons:

- They make you look good.
- They get more done.
- They create successors for you, allowing you to move up in your organization.
- They help your company meet revenue goals.

However, the most important reason to hire top performers, as opposed to low-level performers, is that **poor performers take up to four times the effort to manage as top performers and they produce one fourth the work..**

Once you identify that someone is not a good performer, you need to get them out of your organization, because you will spend inordinate amounts of time managing that poor performer. It's much better to have a team of top performers that need little management to be extremely successful.

Understanding Top Talent

Let's invest a few moments to discuss several models that effectively characterize our target. I did not invent any of the models that we will discuss in the next few pages. As a student of talent and a hunter of top performers I have studied these models. Together they form a story that can help us see the signs of potential in those few candidates who truly are top performers. Success leaves clues, so let's study it.

The Top Twenty Percent Theory

What do top performers look like? Jack Welch of GE fame popularized a model for looking at performance within an organization.[1] This model was composed of three groups: the top twenty percent, middle seventy percent, and bottom ten percent. He went on to describe each of these categories.

The top twenty percent is where we're focused. This group is characterized by extremely high performance. Individuals that fall into this group typically get more done than is asked of them. They're high achievers that are intrinsically motivated to achieve more than others. If you can successfully target this group of individuals, create attractive opportunities for them, and motivate them to want to work for you, you will radically improve your hiring success.

This is the shift you need to make. Throwing out a wide net and hoping a great candidate will come by doesn't work. It's like fishing. If you want to catch a really nice Bluefin tuna in the Pacific Ocean, which strategy would you choose? You might take the time to identify where the fish are, look for the signs of a school and drop your nice fresh bait right into the middle of it. Another option would be to take an old beat up piece of bait and throw it in the big blue ocean and wait for the right fish to come along and take your bait. A well-prepared captain of a tuna boat knows where to go, what to look for, and he always has good fresh bait. And of course, he always comes back with the best fish, sashimi grade Bluefin!

What defines a top performer? Top performers strive for more. They want to take on more, do more, accomplish more, and gain more responsibility. They yearn to have more impact in their organization. These individuals can be easily bored and often look for increased responsibility every two to three years. When given a task, top performers do more than what you ask them to do. They do it with little or no guidance, and they do it better, faster, more efficiently.

These high performers have choices and they are in demand. Top twenty percenters are also smart, articulate, and good communicators. They rarely have to look for a job. If they do, they get multiple job offers. Typically, top performers get an offer for almost every job they interview for. If you want to hire one, you need to work differently and acknowledge that these folks are different. It's also important to understand the other two categories.

The middle seventies make up the majority of any organization. These are people who come to work every day and do a pretty good job, an okay job. If they're managed properly, given the right direction, they might resemble a top twenty percenter. The difference is: the top twenty percenters—you can't keep them down. You don't need to manage them that much. They get it done.

The middle seventies need management. With management intervention, some middle seventies can become top twenties. These folks are the bread and butter and the core of your organization. Some people you think are going to be top twenties might end up being middle seventies and that's okay. You need these people in your organization. They're really valuable employees. I am not saying you should not hire these people, but the purpose of this book is to give you the tools and perspective you need to aim high. By aiming high you will get much better hires. If you are aiming high and have a miss you will still likely end up on the target rather than miss completely and hire a dud.

The bottom ten percent are the duds. These employees are not valuable people in your organization. They are poor performers. They might be in the wrong job; they may lack the skills or experience to do what you need them to do. They commonly lack motivation or have personal issues that get in the way of their performance. These folks are in the wrong job or in the wrong organization. They need to be managed out in a humane, professional way and moved along to a role or an organization that's a better fit for them, where they can be successful

Jack Welch practiced this in his organization. He identified many folks who were managed out of GE as bottom tens and went on to find new productive roles within other organizations or find other careers where they could perform at much more acceptable levels. Don't feel bad for these people. You're doing them a service by helping them identify the right role where they can have an impact.

However useful the top twenty percent model is, it's incomplete. In order to make great hires we must examine and understand two additional frameworks that will round out our perspective.

Headhunter's Secret: Experience Matters

The best headhunters know that making great hires is most assured when you can "poach" talent from a competitor. Hiring people doing the exact same job, in the same industry is the recipe for radical hiring success. The HR jargon for this is: Past and present performance predict future performance. The trick is being able to attract these people, because doing the same exact job in a different organization may lack appeal to the top ten percenters.

There is a theory called stretch hiring, which claims that good people are good no matter what they do. While this may be true, the term "good people" is contextual. When high-performing individuals are placed in roles where they lack experience or skill, they won't be successful.

Here's an example. A leader took an Information Technology (IT) person and moved them into the leadership role of supply chain, and took a Project Management person with some IT experience and put them into the CIO role. Eighteen months later, they were both gone. The supply chain organization was left in shambles with high turnover and IT lost several of its key employees.

Taking a highly successful person from one role and putting him into another, very different role increases your odds of failure. As a professional recruiter, I always advise against this. Instead, find people who have the skills and are doing the job at a competitor, and recruit them. Or develop people in your organization by giving them more responsibility in areas where they can leverage their strengths.

The bottom line is to recruit a top performer doing the same role for a competitor, unless you're hiring for an entry level position that is so new or so specialized that the skills do not exist. You can't just drop in top performers; they must have specific attributes that will make them successful in your role. They must have the right combination of traits, competencies, and experience.

Traits and Competencies

Ok, it's time for some HR mumbo jumbo. I will try my best to simplify the HR speak. The most useful work on a competency model for business was done by Lominger. The model and accompanying books were acquired by Kornferry several years back. This is a very good resource to help you plan your hiring. (For more information visit: http://www.lomingercpm.com) I am not an expert on this model and the intent here is not to give you a deep understanding of HR theory, but rather a brief overview of Traits and Competencies so that we can have a language to discuss the hiring profile.

Trait. Personality traits are often ingrained. Traits are characteristics people have had for most of their lives. They tend to be deep-seated and difficult to learn or unlearn. Examples of traits are things like work ethic, attention to detail, and attitude.

Competency. Competencies are typically a mix of behaviors and skills. If you have strong leadership competencies, it's understood that you may have behavior patterns that are strengthened by certain skills you have developed over time. Generally, competencies are measures of how well you do certain things, taking into consideration your knowledge, skills, and attributes. Competencies are generally behaviors that are easily identified and measured. Think of these as job-related skills such as software, leadership, or other technical skills.

The best practice in defining the job you're hiring for is to focus 80% on traits and 20% on competencies. This helps you avoid being too focused on technical skills and reduces your risk of hiring individuals who lack the interpersonal and leadership skills to be successful.

A Simple Tool to Define Success

Lominger cards are a powerful tool to align yourself and your organization on key competencies. Each card represents a competency and provides a few key phrases that describe that competency.

To purchase a set of Lominger Cards: http://store.kornferry.com/store/lominger/en_US/pd/ThemeID.2815600/productID.152409700?resid=V-ejeQoydBAAAINBGQ-4AAABX&rests=1475847031585. They are now called Leadership Architect® Sort Card Deck by Kornferry, but the Lominger concept remains the same.

The cards are designed to be partnered with a book called *FYI: For Your Improvement*,[2] which explains each competency in more detail. The book also provides ways to assess each competency in order to understand when it's going well and when it's potentially overused. The cards can be an effective, practical, and simple tool to identify and articulate competencies for yourself, your interview team and the broader organization.

First, review the deck and identify the competencies that are the most important for your role. Set that pile aside. Then select cards that are clearly competencies that don't resonate or aren't needed. The most effective way to do this is to think about people that you know in your organization or in organizations you've worked for in the past. What people are highly effective in the role you're trying to fill? Identify the competencies that align with what you know about these people.

Your list will probably be too long. Prioritize and shorten it. Ultimately, you should land on no more than three to five competencies. Vet them and select the ones that are most important. Often, there's just a small nuance between them, so try to align them by category. Your goal is to land on three or four. Three is ideal.

The second method is to focus on the competencies within your organization. This approach requires a buy in from the organization. If you're running a larger team or you're looking for complementary skills, you can use your own group or a focus group to identify the competencies that you want to drive towards. The benefit of this approach is that you get different views. You can still use the approach of identifying highly effective or top performing individuals in your organization. Consider the things a group does well and what skills you might want to add. You will benefit by including someone in the group who brought those competencies into the organization.

Once you identify the traits and competencies that would

benefit you and your team most, incorporate this information into your hiring profile.

Complementary Skills

Rob Reindl, the former head of HR for Edwards Lifesciences and the author of *The How of Leadership,*[3] put a high value on complementary skills. (I was fortunate to have this great leader as my mentor.) People with complementary skills are team members whose views, opinions, and skills are different from yours. For example, I'm a horrible speller, which is funny because I'm the author of two business books. Between books, articles, blog posts and job descriptions, I probably write around 10,000 words a week.

To be successful, I need to surround myself with people with complementary skills, people who are very detailed oriented. As a strategic visionary person, I like to think about the big picture and set big, audacious goals. So, it's important to surround myself and hire people who have a dominant practical and realistic side. People who are focused on how we're going to get this done. What does that look like? What are the steps? This makes for a highly effective team. The tendency of many leaders is to hire people just like themselves, and what that creates is group think. If you have a person who agrees with everything you say and doesn't see your flat sides, your team will not be optimized.

Critical Learnings:

In order to create radical hiring success, you must:

- Target top twenty percenters as the focus of your

hiring strategy (more on how to do this in the next chapter).

- Identify the Traits and Competencies that will lead to success in the role you need to hire.
- Find people with the most relevant experience and a track record of delivering.
- Build a team with complementary skills.

Putting Planning into action

In order to attract the right talent, you must apply the principles you've learned: Define your talent gap and develop a few key tools to support your success. The goal of this effort is to deliver two documents:

- A well composed and targeted Job Description.
- A One Page critical skills profile with candidate messaging.

First, toss out all the paperwork from HR including all the old job descriptions. These are just boilerplate forms that will clutter your process and distract you from your goal.

Take out a blank piece of paper and brainstorm. Paint a picture of what the job is, why it's important, the type of individual you believe can accomplish the tasks, and why someone desires the job. Once you've completed your brainstorming/discovery process, creating these documents is easy. It's the brainstorming that's hard. Using a framework will help.

Deliverables

Challenge yourself to think in terms of deliverables instead of responsibilities. Responsibilities are boring, create mediocre expectations, and are generally not attractive to a top performer. After all, if we are looking to attract a motivated, success-minded individual who's doing the same job at a competitor, telling them all about the same job they are already doing will not be too exciting. To define the deliverables, use the vision approach.

Vision Exercise

Imagine yourself walking down the hallway 12 months from now with your new employee. This person has just had an amazing year and you're about to give her a stellar review and a nice big bonus.

- What has she accomplished?
- Why was it important?
- How did she do it?
- What was the impact on you, the company, and her career of getting these important things done?

Here are some additional questions to ask yourself as you identify the deliverables:

1. What do you want this person to accomplish in the first 90 days, 6 months and one year?
2. How will doing this job impact each of the following areas?
   a. You?
   b. The new hire?
   c. Your team?
   d. The company?
   e. Society?

3. Do you have people in your group doing a job like this or in the company?
   a. Who are the top performers? (Keep this information handy for discussion in the next chapter.)
   b. What is it about them that makes them so successful?
4. Have you worked with people like this at another company?
   a. Who are the top performers? (Keep this information handy for discussion in the next chapter.)
   b. What is it about them that makes them so successful?
5. What are the most important technical skills for the role (Competencies)?
6. Define the critical soft skills (Traits).

When we talk about the top twenty percent, middle seventy, and bottom ten, the emphasis is on attitude, motivation, work ethic, and values, not technical expertise. I don't mean you should hire a bunch of inexperienced people and expect them to be successful. They must have some basic business experience that is relevant to the job. But what's most important is that they have the right traits, the pieces in their character that will make them successful.

Also, consider complementary skills:

- What skills or experience would complement your team?
- What skills do you need?

Selling Points or WIFM

The third, final and most critical factor in attracting radically successful talent is to ask the following question. Why would someone want to quit their job and accept yours? Or for that matter, invest the time to interview with you?

It's time to sell your job, and the first rule of sales is to explain the obvious. Just because you think the job is great doesn't mean other people will see it that way. Explain why your position is interesting or exciting to a top performer. Focus on specific things that are unique or compelling about the role. Many companies work on exciting products and are growing so you need to get very detailed here. What is driving your growth, why is the product exciting?

Questions to ask:

1. What is special or unique about this role?
2. Why would someone quit their job and want to do this job?
3. If done well what could this position lead to?
4. Who will this position impact and how will it impact them?
5. What gets you out of bed each morning and excited to come to work?
6. Why would someone go work for your company and not a competitor?
7. What's special, different, or exciting about your company?

Job Descriptions

This is the place where many, many leaders fail. I can't tell you how many times I've been called in to fix recruitment processes. Not infrequently, jobs have been open for many months and in a few cases over a year. The first place I always started wasn't the most exciting. It was the job description. Overall, these job descriptions were horrible and I could see why they could not attract top performers.

You can have the most technical role, the biggest requirements, but if nobody wants to do your job, then you'll never fill it. You will end up with a hole in your organization.

An effective job description aligns your interview team. It's not only important that you understand what you're looking to hire and why someone would want this job. It's extremely critical that the people in your organization understand it as well. All the stakeholders need to be included. If your HR partner is going to interview the people, that person needs to know what you're looking for and what's attractive about this job. If you have an interview team—which all of you will have after reading this book—they're going to need to know too. And if you have a recruiter, an internal recruiter or a headhunter, passing along this information to them should be No. 1 on your list.

The final reason to have this job description is the impact on your candidates. We all know that many people respond well to verbal information. They want to hear what's exciting about a job, they want to hear what this job will lead to, but others will respond better to the written word. People who are more detail-oriented, who are more visual in their learning style, need to see it in writing.

Let's look at two examples of job descriptions to highlight what we are attempting to accomplish.

Example of typical job description: Where are the selling points?

Research and Development Engineer

ESSENTIAL DUTIES AND RESPONSIBILITIES:

- Design state of the art high density electronic subsystems for new and existing products.
- Perform electronic circuit and system simulation analysis.
- Develop board layouts and create schematics and drawings.
- Develop test and debug embedded software for digital applications.
- Develop manufacturing embedded and windows MFC software for production ready products.
- Prepare time and cost estimates for designs and projects.
- BOM development and component selection for cost sensitive assemblies.
- Develop Intellectual property through proper research and documentation.
- Technically support cross functional engineering groups on test and build requirements.
- Effectively use an advanced Product Development Process.
- Develop products to the latest applicable IEC, FDA and international regulatory requirements.
- Write engineering test protocols for component parts and integrated systems.

- Be responsible for design control verification, validation, process validation and design reviews.
- Support supplier research, selection and qualification for components and subassemblies.
- Work with Manufacturing Engineering to plan and execute Design for Manufacturability and Design for Testability for all electronic subassemblies.
- Assist product transfers from product development to manufacturing.
- Support the design, development and selection of manufacturing and test equipment.
- Coordinate efforts with Quality Assurance to document and support regulatory requirements & filings.

EDUCATION:

- Bachelor's degree in Electrical Engineering

EXPERIENCE:

- Ten (10) years' experience in analog, digital and embedded/Windows development software design and product development.

REQUIRED SKILLS:

- Expert level digital/analog design skills.
- ARM microcontroller and EPROM design application experience.
- Proficiency with electrical design software tools (Orcad schematic capture and PCB layout).
- Must be able to develop, debug, test and document

application software and systems that contain logical and mathematical controls.

- Knowledge of printed circuit board fabrication and circuit card assembly processes.
- Ability to use lab equipment such as oscilloscopes and spectrum analyzers.
- Ability to write engineering documents, test protocols, laboratory notebook entries, and reports.
- Experience with Signal Conditioning, Active Filters, Electrical Isolation.
- Strong EMI/EMC design compatibility experience.
- Ability to breadboard, test, and debug prototype electronics and software based systems.
- Ability to perform component engineering design changes.
- Plan, write, and execute comprehensive hardware and software verification plans.
- Generate hardware and software subsystem requirement documents.
- Experience in the design of motion control devices and/or motor interface electronics.
- Demonstrated history of successfully completed products or projects.

Example of an Improved Job Description

DESCRIPTION:

ABC Company is undergoing explosive growth and investing heavily in R&D and Clinical Trials.

We innovate and develop XYZ products and bring

them to market to LMNOP. ABC Company is seeking an individual with a unique combination of skills and a desire to impact the treatment of ABC which affects more than 33 million people worldwide and predisposes them to a five-fold increased risk of stroke.

ABC Company's success in the marketplace has been the result of a commitment to the science behind its products and the ability to bring the right solutions to market in a timely fashion.

You will join a nimble Research and Technology team that operates in a pre-design control environment. We evaluate technology white space, identify unmet needs, develop concepts, build and test quick-turn prototypes, and work with clinicians to improve a design before transitioning it to our Product Development Teams.

Within the first year, you will prototype and code an XYZ, work with a multidisciplinary team to develop a small, maneuverable LMNOP, investigate and develop prototypes using a novel energy modality for ablating tissue, and develop multiphysics models of RF interaction with ACX.

ABC Company offers dual-path opportunities for Engineers and Scientists to grow. The technical path moves from Primary through Senior Fellow. We are highly supportive of the development of Intellectual Property and of attending pertinent medical conferences. We also have a "Ride with a Rep" program to bring you into close interaction with clinicians in operating rooms and hybrid suites.

POSITION SUMMARY:

The successful candidate will have a strong track record of innovation. They will be comfortable collaborating with clinicians to identify unmet needs and solutions. They will lead research activities and exercise independent judgment to clarify and prioritize tasks to facilitate decision making. Additionally, they will provide technical expertise as a member of an agile, multidisciplinary team of Scientists, Engineers, and Model Makers. The successful candidate will be comfortable designing and implementing integrated solutions that include digital, analog, and software elements. The ability to work with consultants and suppliers to implement solutions will be required.

ROLES AND RESPONSIBILITIES:

- Define requirements, build, test and implement a platform for developing and evaluating novel ablation algorithms.
- Lead efforts to identify and optimize novel RF ablation algorithms using rapidly modifiable software, such as LabView.
- Lead efforts to develop and validate a model of the physical interaction of RF energy and tissue using multiphysics software such as COMSOL or ANSYS.
- Develop relationships with Key Opinion Leaders in the cardiothoracic surgery, cardiology, and electrophysiology fields that lead to identification of opportunities and co-invention of devices.

- Participate in Voice of the Customer planning, collection, and analysis.
- Plan and conduct hands-on experimental work (bench, in vitro and in vivo) to fully evaluate device prototypes.
- Collaborate with Product Development teams to efficiently transition projects/concepts into Design Control.
- Prepare presentations and reports in support of R&D activities. Create clear informative communications in PowerPoint. Present research opportunities, technology concepts, test data, and provide recommendations to management.
- Submit new innovations regularly to Patent Review Board.
- Stay abreast of latest relevant technology through literature, seminars, conferences, academia, and industry.

BASIC QUALIFICATIONS:

- BSEE + 15 years of experience, or MSEE + 10 years of experience or PhD + 5 years of experience in electrical engineering.
- Significant experience identifying medical device unmet needs and developing, prototyping, and testing concepts to address those needs.
- Experience in applying analog, digital, and software solutions in medical device research.
- Demonstrated initiative to solve complex technical problems.

- Track record of successful product development working in cross-functional project teams.
- Outstanding written and verbal communication skills.
- Track record of generating intellectual property.
- Experience with LabView/MatLab.

As you can see from the examples, if you take the candidate's perspective, one job description is a laundry list of tasks and requirements while the other is a motivational document that inspires a vision of what the job is, what the candidate could become and the impact they will have. If you were choosing between the two roles, what would your choice be?

Beyond the Job Description - One Pager

Now that you have created an attractive, interesting and compelling job description you are well on your way to attracting radically successful talent. The next step is to go beyond 99% of your competitors and develop a simple document that will allow you and your interview team to boil it down to the essentials.

This one page position profile will allow you to make faster, better decisions, align your interview team, and sell candidates on your job.

This doesn't have to be a super fancy thing. It doesn't need to be a complex evaluation form. This tool should identify the three most critical skills along with major selling points in an easy to read and readily available format. Specifically, a short bulleted list of the critical characteristics and attributes that you're looking for in the person that you want to hire for the position. In addition, I suggest that you also create a list of your selling points or talking points about why someone would want to do this position.

This is the tool you can use when you prepare your interview team and when you debrief after your interview. Creating a simple "one pager" will allow you and the team to be accountable to simple objectives. This document allows you to be very specific about what you're looking for in the person you hire. You can't always be that specific in your job description as it's focused on candidates. You need one document for public distribution and one for internal alignment. If you're too specific on what you distribute publicly you can end up with people who manipulate the system and pretend they are what you want. These two documents should align. It's not like you're looking for different things, it's just that you need to be careful about how much you reveal traits publicly.

Separate it out and keep some of the personality targets on your internal document only. This will keep people from "playing the part".

Example Position Profile

Role: Plant Manager

Critical Skills

- Charismatic leader
  - Plant is going through significant change
  - Need an individual people will follow
  - Takes time to get to know people

- Credible business leader
  - Trust between plant and corporate is poor; need person who can build trust
  - Communication metrics
  - Understands how to manage executive expectations
- Industry Experience
  - Experience in ABC industry
  - Needs to understand XYZ regulations

Selling Points

- The ABC plant is the largest and most important in our company
  - Highly visible role - get noticed by our CEO
  - Could lead to VP Operations positions
- Our products help people
  - Feel good about what you do
  - Leave a legacy
- As the largest manufacturing plant in ABC we create the most jobs
  - Position seen as a local leader
  - Highly respected
  - Success in plant means more jobs and helping more local families
- Our Culture – people focused, fun, flexible
  - Low bureaucracy – less frustrating to work here
  - Fun people to work with - feels like a family, not a job

CHAPTER 3:
Develop a Targeted Approach to Find Great Candidates

As we know, most top performers are actively working and well taken care of. This one fact should help explain why many of the candidates HR sends you or who have applied to your job are not very good. They are fishing from a pool that is mostly populated with "B and C players." In order to maximize your probability of making a radically successful hire it's important to focus your efforts. The majority of your pipeline needs to come from individuals who are actively engaged in a role doing work similar to what you're looking for. By making this your focus you'll increase the probability of picking a top twenty percenter.

There are three critical steps you need to master this strategy:

- Understand where the best candidates come from.
- Lead the development and execution of a strategy to target top performers.
- Network and build your professional brand.

Mommy, Where Do Top Performers Come From?

Many of us have had to respond to a similar question from

our kids. Fortunately, the answer as to where great candidates come from is simpler and less uncomfortable. Now that you have invested the time to read the previous chapter, you have taken a significant step in understanding where top performing candidates come from. Simply put, the top performing people are at your competitors. Attracting them means convincing people who are happy and not looking for a position to consider your job because it's a better opportunity than the one they have today.

There's another major principle of successful recruiting. Candidates leave leaders to go to other leaders. They don't leave companies or jobs, they leave poor leaders to go to work for better, more inspiring ones. Become one of those leaders and you'll instantly be more attractive. Once you accept this fact, things become simpler.

Leading the Development and Execution of a Strategy to Target Top Performers

As a leader, one of your prime responsibilities is to drive the attraction of talent. You have three choices here. You can either roll up your sleeves and start networking by contacting people on LinkedIn. Second, you can hire a recruiter and a headhunter to do the work for you, or third, you can have the internal HR team do that work. What's important among these choices is that you focus on high-performing individuals working at competitors and know how to track the folks that are likely not looking.

In order to hire great people, you must take responsibility for leading the strategy to find them. Become an educated consumer of the recruitment process. As with many tasks in leadership, asking the right questions and driving the right strategy yield big results. You will also need to develop the skills to recruit/attract (SELL) that top performer. Don't worry, we cover that in chapter five.

Stop Focusing on Job Applicants

A key strategy to drive the quality of your pipeline is to build the pool of candidates you target, not candidates who "apply" to your job. That's why resources like ZipRecruiter who advertise all over the place aren't the best source. If you want to have more applicants that aren't qualified, post your job in more places.

If you want to have more people who will be successful in your organization and create accomplishments that help propel you in your career, you need to attract people who aren't looking for jobs. Many full time professional recruiters don't understand this critical fact; it's a major reason why there are so many bad recruiters.

There's another advantage to this strategy. Attracting people who aren't looking for a job puts you in a situation to have less competition. It's like looking at a house before it goes on the market. People who are looking for jobs tend to look for jobs at multiple companies. If they are any good—and statistics show that only a small percentage of applicants are good—then they're going to get offers from every company they interview with. If you're able to attract candidates who aren't looking for a job, which is essentially creating your own candidates, ones who are working and engaged in their job but are open to something better and are interested in working for one of the top authorities in their field, a great leader like yourself, then you're not going to have competition. It's not about hiring. It's about working out a deal between two professionals that supports the other professional to meet his career goals and allows you to meet yours. That's a win-win, and there's little competition when you're in that type of situation.

Targeted Efforts Are Critical

Most managers want a greater number of candidates regardless of where they come from, in the belief that more equals better. I recommend that you focus on the quality of candidates rather than the quantity. Make sure your recruiting actions are targeted to get you the right candidates.

Get into the details by asking this question: "Where are these candidates coming from and what are we doing to get more and better ones?" By focusing on this one aspect you'll automatically get higher quality candidates targeted to your specific profile.

Get Hands On

Many leaders take a far too hands-off approach to the building of a pipeline and rely on others to do it. Becoming educated enough to ask the right questions about what's being done and how it's being done is critical to identifying the right caliber of talent. Regardless of your level, whether you're a CEO or a manager hiring your first person, you need to take accountability and ask the right questions.

Avoid Making Yourself Look Desperate

Another common mistake of leaders is to use multiple

recruiters and create a "horse race." In this approach, the manager doesn't care who works on the job or how it gets done. They just call a bunch of recruiters and hope that by putting more resources on the problem, it will be solved. The problem is, they don't understand the issue. The issue is that the best candidates aren't looking. Having more people call the best candidates or call the same candidates that are looking, doesn't solve the problem. The solution to the problem is focused effort and good salesmanship. You need resources that will be able to convince those targeted candidates who aren't looking that your job, your management, and your company is worth looking at.

Use Only the Best Recruiters

Simply having more unskilled, mediocre sales people call and leave annoying and harassing voicemails, send emails, or botched presentations, doesn't improve your chances of getting a great candidate. All it does is make you appear desperate, pollute the market with an impure message or poorly delivered message, and poison the pool for the candidates that you want. Remember, per our sniper philosophy, we only need one good candidate. And if that one good candidate has been called eight times by eight different recruiters, and told eight different messages that weren't even that good, they're never going to come interview for you.

The problem is that many recruiters don't headhunt any more. It's a lost, dying art that's been replaced by low quality, mudslinging corporate recruiters, search guys who are lazy and don't understand the business. Posting a job online or trolling LinkedIn isn't headhunting. Headhunting is taking the time to learn a market, develop a database of the best people and build relationships with them. There are no shortcuts here. The best headhunters take years to develop. Next year, I am going to publish a book to help these folks get back on track and recruit great talent, but for now, just recognize not all recruiters are headhunters. Find the ones who are and work with them.

What's the Deal With Recruiters?

In my previous book, I discuss the different types of recruiters and how they can help people with their career. Let's invest a few minutes exploring how they can help you hire. There are two classifications of recruiters, internal recruiters and headhunters.

The Pros and Cons of Internal Recruiters

Internal recruiters are the recruiters that your company employs to handle your open jobs. The advantage of these folks is that you're not paying any additional external fees for this person. The cost to a company for this type of resource is fixed, typically you pay them a salary or hourly rate without any commission so the cost is the same regardless of how many people you hire. The other advantage is they know the culture of your organization and what type of people work best in it. The disadvantage is that these folks tend to have a very high workload. This means they have little time to reach out and attract candidates that aren't looking for a job. The typical strategy of an internal recruiting model is to have fewer recruiters working on more job openings.

I spent ten years managing an internal recruitment program and I'm one of the few people in the entire recruitment business book-writing industry that has worked in both internal corporate recruiting and as a headhunter. Based on this experience, I can tell you that internal recruiters are extremely cost-effective; however, they struggle to find the top performers from your competitors. Internal recruiting works best when you're hiring many very similar jobs and candidates aren't hard to find.

Their tools tend to be limited to things like LinkedIn, candidate applicants, and possibly a little bit of networking if they have any time. There is little focus on the proactive and strategic parts of recruitment. I estimate that most spend less than five percent of their time speaking to people in the industry who aren't looking for a job. That simply isn't an effective model. If this model works for you, that's just great. But if you need to find a star in a shorter period, your best options are: A, to take matters into your own hands and reach out to people in your network or build your own network or, B, get somebody to do the job who's already built a network of high quality candidates in your industry.

Are External Recruiters Better?

Since I run an external recruiting firm, you might be thinking that I am now going to tell you how great external recruiters are. Unfortunately, most headhunters now work more like corporate recruiters or worse, they are pushy sales people with zero knowledge. They work on LinkedIn, they post jobs, they send whatever they find. Become an educated consumer and learn where the experts reside. These are the individuals who can help you to target top performers, and coach you to make you a better hiring manger.

How the Best Recruiters Work

If you ask the right questions within your network and interview recruiters, you'll discover that not all recruiters spend all their time on LinkedIn. Some recruiters work in the old-school way that existed before LinkedIn when the telephone, a database, and printed directories were the only way to find talent. They pick up the phone. They strive to identify people who are happy in their job and not looking. They build relationships and market knowledge which allows them to create candidates that don't exist by identifying gaps in individuals' career goals and offer new opportunity to fill in those gaps.

This skill takes years to develop and isn't in the toolkit of most corporate recruiters. It simply doesn't make sense for them to do this. Headhunters need to build relationships with all good candidates across geographies and functions within their market. Corporate recruiters don't place the same value on building relationships in their industry. They're focused on their company and candidates they can hire now to fill current jobs. From a candidate's perspective, they also have little need to befriend a corporate recruiter unless they are looking for a job at their company. A headhunter can unlock many, many doors so it's wise to get to know a few. Candidates know this, so the smart ones are more likely to speak to you even if they're not looking.

This is the power that a truly effective headhunter brings to your career and the power that a headhunter brings to your search process.

Ask How Recruiters Work

Unfortunately, this is the era of the "Lazy LinkedIn Recruiter." Why anyone would pay twenty or thirty thousand dollars for a headhunter who posts jobs or trolls LinkedIn is beyond me. This investment only makes sense when you hire a market expert who has invested the time to build their own network and a highly valuable database. Sure, I use LinkedIn but I use it as a source for data not as my major focus. Find a recruiter who is focused on finding people that aren't looking for a job and your investment will be well worth it.

I'm not saying that you need to use search for all your jobs. The fact is you may be able to build a network and relationships that allow you to identify top quality talent with little to no use of headhunters. However, when that's not working, before you go post and pray, and hope that somebody applies for your job, consider using the expertise of a headhunter that knows and works in your marketplace to get you connected with talent that can change the game for you.

Creating Pipelines That Matter

Much is said in this information-packed age about pipelines, sourcing, social media, and talent pools. At the end of the day, as a business leader responsible for hiring radically successful talent, none of this business gibberish matters.

What you need to do is surround yourself with high-performing individuals. This isn't the fanciest strategy, but it's the one that works. *"Eagles soar with eagles and turkeys hobble around on the ground with other turkeys."*

Although there are exceptions to every rule, it's unlikely to find the top performer hanging out with a bunch of duds. So, get to know the top performers in your organization and they'll give you an accurate view of who is high performing in other organizations and in yours.

The Power of Networking to Identify Great Talent

If you boil down what great headhunters do to its essence, it's just basic networking. What you're paying for is the network they have developed to circumvent the time factor for you. What is networking really? Networking is about developing mutually beneficial relationships where you get help from other people and you help them.

Networking Inside Your Company

A great place to start networking is with top performers inside your company. They likely know other top performers from other companies they have worked at. The ask goes something like this:

"Hey, I want to build my network because I'm doing some hiring. Who are the best [insert name of position or role, or challenge]? Who is the best person at designing X, Y, Z widgets that you've ever worked with?"

The person might say, "Why? Joe's never going to leave."

Your response: "I just want to build a network because people like Joe probably know other high performing people."

Networking is often about putting the other person's needs first. It's about helping them. Invite someone to lunch or coffee or have a quick networking call or discussion at a face-to-face networking group. People get focused about networking when they need a job, but networking isn't just for getting a job. Becoming active in a networking group can help your career, whether it's the association that industry professionals in your niche belong to or a local group of business executives.

When I say to increase your networking, I don't mean you should target job networking groups. These tend to be populated by the unemployed job seeker and this population is less likely to have top-performing stars since they are typically fully employed and highly engaged.

Great Leaders Attract Great Followers and Mediocre Leaders Struggle to Find People to Work for Them.

Develop yourself first and others will follow. I had a mentor once explain this to me in the following way.

When the plane is about to take off, the stewardesses or stewards come into the middle of the aisle and do their safety briefing. They say something like "In the event of sudden cabin depressurization, masks will drop from above your head. Please secure your mask before securing those of small children traveling with you." In other words, take care of yourself first before you take care of the others.

You can't take care of others if you're incapacitated by lack of oxygen and you can't be a great leader until you've worked on your own leadership skills and your own personal development. Invest in yourself and followers will come.

Build Your Leadership Brand

The second thing you can do to become a more attractive leader is create a brand and publicize yourself. In my first book, *This Book Will Get You Hired for the Job You Want,* I offer valuable advice to job seekers on how to brand themselves as strong candidates. This advice also applies to managers and leaders. To attract great followers, use tools like LinkedIn, Twitter, and other social media apps, as well as in-person networking.

Your "enhanced" network provides a ready source for candidates when you need to hire. Even if you don't have an open position now, you can start building your network. Too many people ignore their brand by being too focused on their job and the internal situation of their organization. Build a network by following the steps outlined in my first book or check out my website MrAdamo.com for free resources.

Get More High Quality Referrals

A healthy network helps you find people through referrals. Another good source of candidates is your own team.

You also can do it by being more visible on LinkedIn. Post more frequently, like people's updates. The more active way is to reach out directly. That doesn't mean saying, "Hey, I'm hiring. Are you looking?" It's more like, "Hey, I'm building my organization and I know you're in the same widget space I am. Who's the best widget guy that you know?" And if you paint an attractive picture of the opportunity, people are going to say, "That sounds phenomenal."

Here's a more specific example you might use in a conversation or email. "Hey, I'm working in the widget space. I manage a team. Our primary goal is to create the best widgets in the world. I have an opportunity on my team for a widget designer and what's exciting about it is that this widget designer is actually going to create a widget that's going to save people's lives and make them live an extra ten years. If they're successful, there's a great career path available. We actually have room for another VP on the team. And so I'm wondering which really good widget designers do you know that I should talk to."

The Do It Yourself Approach

Recruiting passive talent isn't difficult, however it takes time, effort and some practice. As a leader who is focused on advancing your career, you should make recruiting part of what you do every day. Each time you get the opportunity to speak to a potential top performer take the time to plant some seeds.

Actually doing the recruitment when you have a need to hire is a different matter. Recruitment is time consuming so you will need to consider how much time you must invest. At a minimum, you should plan on having some conversations with key individuals. Managers who appreciate the art and science of selling themselves and their organization are almost always in a better position to recruit top talent. In the beginning of a new hire, I often bring a list of prospects to discuss with the VP or manager. We prioritize the prospects and decide who will make the first contact. This highly targeted, personal approach goes a long way in getting someone to "take a look" at an opportunity.

Taglines on LinkedIn and Looking to Hire Postings Rarely Work

Many managers post their job on LinkedIn with an update that says "Looking to Hire." Or they send the job out through an email with the same tag. This is no different than the desperate candidate who posts an update with, "Looking for a Job." Not only are these tags ineffective, they impact the perception of your brand negatively.

Let's review:

- Take accountability for leading the candidate identification strategy.
- Focus on the quality of recruitment activity rather than the quantity of candidates.
- Get into the details of what's being done to contact and attract people at your competitors.
- Build your own professional brand.
- Choose a recruitment strategy that works for your time and budget.

CHAPTER 4:

Design an Interview Process That Attracts, Not Interrogates

In these pages, I will give you simple guidelines to show you how to identify top performing individuals who can impact your organization. By the time you finish this chapter you will never think of your role as an interviewer or interviewing in the same way. Interviewing is typically seen as a horribly unappealing, stressful, and unenjoyable process. It's slightly less stressful for the interviewer than it is for the candidate, but if you're worried about making a poor hiring decision it can be stressful for you too.

Active candidates who are looking for a job are more likely to make themselves sound more appealing than people who aren't looking for a position. Employed candidates are easy to interview, sure they may be a bit standoffish at first, but they have little motivation to lie or embellish because they already have a job and they may not be that interested. On the other hand, people out of work may be smooth and practiced at making themselves sound better than they are, so be vigilant.

Regardless of where candidates come from, focus on creating a process that helps you hire great people. To accomplish this goal, you need three critical components, or as I call them, the three A's:

- **Assess** - Determine if the person is a high performing individual capable of being successful in the role you want to hire.
- **Attract** - Provide an experience and give information that attracts high performing individuals.
- **Accelerate** – Create a process that moves quickly enough to "sweep the candidate off his feet."

Most interviews focus on assessment and neglect the other two components. This is a huge missed opportunity. If you have an interview strategy that is too heavily weighted on assessment, you risk ending up with bad hires. Many managers believe that assessment is the key to a good hire, but it's simply not true. Targeting is the key to good hires; assessment, attraction and acceleration allow that targeting to work.

If your strategy is to "weed out" poor applicants rather than to identify top performers, then yes, assessment is your key, but your chance of making a bad hire is around 50% because interviews never tell the whole story. It's more effective to target and attract top performers but it takes focus and hard work. You can do it!

Implementing an Assess, Attract, and Accelerate Interview Strategy

Managers spend a lot of time developing and implementing assessments in the attempt to screen down candidates and only identify the ones that they want for the job. Unfortunately, most assessments are no better than 50-50. At the end of the day, you're basing a decision on a very thin snapshot of a person in a highly prepared and unrealistic way, and trying to make assumptions about his/her performance in the future. Your likelihood of making a great hire is much higher if you focus on an individual who's working for a competitor and who already has a long track record of accomplishments that align with your goals.

You will need to adjust your assessment approach to allow each individual to highlight his experience and accomplishments in a natural way and allow you to figure out if he is a top performer or if he is just giving you well-prepared interview responses. You must spend more time listening than you do interrogating.

Attraction

You need to build attraction into each step of your interview process. Once you recognize that an individual is somebody you want to recruit, you need to invest time talking about what's great about your job, your company, your organization, and working for you.

Most people spend little to no time speaking about what attracts candidates because they incorrectly assume the people they are interviewing are looking for a job. This can't be further from the truth. With the current market conditions, top performers always have choices. You want them to choose you.

How to Create Attraction

Think about what gets you excited about your job. Each day there's something that gets you out of bed and looking forward to work. If not, you need to read my first book and get the job you want. But assuming that you're in a job you want, it's easy to think about the things that excite you.

Number two, think about what this position could lead to if done well. Most people tend to hedge everything with "Well, for the right person and if this goes well…" but what's important is to have a powerful, positive vision. You're not out to hire the wrong person. You're not out to hire the middle achiever. You're out to hire the top performer. If you don't outline what will happen for the high achiever, you'll never attract the high achiever. The high achiever doesn't seek to be mediocre. They're not interested in a position where they can just bump along. They're interested in a position and an opportunity that will let them achieve their career goals. In order to attract individuals like this, you must talk about what the position will lead to and make an assumption that you're hiring a top performer.

By incorporating this approach in each interview, you'll create an experience people want to be a part of. They'll want to work for you. They'll want to join your team. Top performers have choices and you want them to choose you.

Identifying Top Performers

It's actually pretty simple and goes back to a principle I learned in my first days of recruiter training back in the late 90s at MRI. Past performance predicts future performance. That means that the people who will do an extremely good job for your organization have the traits of high-performing individuals. They're self-motivated, confident, focused on achieving, driven internally to succeed and to exceed your expectations. They have the competencies that you're looking for. That is to say, they have the skills to do the job you want. In order to know they have the skills to do the job you want, they have to have already done the job you want or at least parts of it.

As we discussed in the earlier chapter on planning, part of the art is to identify what those skills are, those competencies that we absolutely, positively must have. That list should be relatively short. Remember, the competencies are only a small component of what we're looking for here. Nevertheless, many interviewing guides focus solely on how to identify these competencies by creating a long list of questions and highly structured interviews. The secret that all good recruiters know is that interviewing isn't about a long list of questions. Interviewing is about people and understanding them, their motivations, and their experience.

By creating too much clutter, we impede our ability to listen and hear the answers that are there. High performance leaves footprints, breadcrumbs we can follow on the path to hiring a high performing individual. These breadcrumbs are otherwise known as accomplishments. Accomplishments are things that you get done that impact an organization. They save the company money. They increase sales. They reduce time to complete something. High performers have a long list of accomplishments. Think of your own organization, what separates you from others?

As I tell candidates, "Joe Schmo, the poor performing engineer, could have the exact same list of responsibilities as you, the high performing person. What separates you from Joe Schmo is your accomplishments, the things you got done." We need to understand past accomplishments and make sure that this person completed those accomplishments, what he did, how he did it. We will also need to understand what motivates him. This powerful combination of experience and future motivation unlocks a treasure trove of information about the individual that you're interviewing. In order to do this, you must have a clear profile of the position. This is why step one in this process is so important. You must know what you're looking for, so when you interview this person you can key in on what those components are. This also creates a more interesting and engaging conversation.

Stop Interrogating and Start Listening to Candidates

I once worked with a manager who had a very long list of questions. He thought he was quite effective at interviewing. He listed those questions on his computer and when the candidate would come in for an interview, he'd say, "Excuse me," turn his back to face the computer behind his desk where the candidate was sitting and proceed to read those questions to the candidate, and take meticulous notes. All the while, his back was turned to the candidate. It was like an interrogation. The only thing that was missing was the bright, white light. However, the manager did a great job of thoroughly assessing the competencies of each individual. He had excellent notes, but the one thing he was missing was any form of relationship. Guess what? Candidates didn't want to work for this person. He also missed key items about the candidate's background because the candidate didn't feel comfortable sharing.

Create a Comfortable and Relaxed Feel for Your Interviews

Candidates immediately become defensive when they feel interrogated. When everything's being written down, it's natural for them to think, "This is on the record. I have to be careful what I say." When you create an easy, comfortable interviewing environment that feels unstructured and informal, candidates get comfortable. And when candidates get comfortable, their real personalities, traits, and competencies come out. Be well-prepared and know what you're interested in. Ask questions and follow-up those questions with thoughtful and curious questions.

Behavioral Interviewing Sounds Fancy, But It's Simple

In order to implement this, we use the behavioral interview strategy. You can read more about behavioral interviewing in a wide variety of texts. Probably the best behavioral interviewing resource that I've come across is Interview Edge, www.interviewedge.com. They offer training as well as online courses and manuals. They'll come out to your company and train your employees. I've worked with Interview Edge for years and I believe that the techniques they teach will help you become more of an effective interviewer. However, don't mistake this for an endorsement for creating a highly structured interview process. Instead, use these techniques to enhance your comfort and skill, and incorporate them into a very relaxed and comfortable interviewing process.

Implementing an Interview Structure That Works

Here's my two-minute version of behavioral interviewing. Behavioral interviewing is basically asking people to give an example of something they did, how they did it, and when they did it. In order to prepare for a behavioral interview with a candidate, you need to review his resume before you meet with him and identify accomplishments that align with the things that you're looking for or that create an interest for you. Then in the interview, you can simply ask, "Tell me about yourself." The first thing you want to do is get to know this person. During this process, listen for accomplishments, motivations, goals, and values. This will tell you a lot about this person. Then take two or three minutes to tell your own career story. This is an important step. Candidates have done their research, but they naturally come in nervous and uncomfortable. Telling your story builds a bond, creates rapport, and creates a level of comfort that allows them to be who they are and get past their scripted interview approach.

Additionally, the people you meet with that you don't hire might be great professional contacts in the future. By telling your story, you've made a connection. You never know how things will break in the future. You may be interviewing with them one day. After you tell your story, begin by asking probing questions about things you're interested in.

"Hey, I see that you had $200 million in sales last year.

Tell me about how you did that. I see that you completed this project ahead of schedule and under budget. What went into that? What was your role and tell me how you did that?"

As you listen to the stories, continue to ask probing questions. Ask for clarification. Avoid structured interview questions. People can prepare for those. Instead, ask casual probing questions. You'll get a really good feel for what this person brings to the table, who they are and how they work. In addition to that, you'll build a relationship with this person and make them feel like you're someone they might want to work with.

If You Like What You Hear, Make a Smooth Transition from Assessing to Selling

If you start to hear things that you like from this person, invest time telling them about why you work for the company, what your career has been like, what your career goals are, and where you see this position leading to. Use all those selling points that we discussed when you first scoped out the position.

Identify and Engage an Effective Interview Team

- Take some time to pick an interview team that will provide honest and well-rounded feedback.
- Your team should be no more than 3 to 5 people, and they should represent a range of perspectives. Don't just pick people that think like you. People with

different experiences and work styles will focus on different things, giving you a broader perspective.

- Invest time in preparing your interview team with a 30-minute call or meeting to review your position profile and key things you're looking for, as well as to determine who should focus on what, in order to provide a more focused interview process and better feedback.

Develop Your Interviewing Skills

Interviewing is a skill—invest time and resources to develop your skills. There are many great training programs and books, so make it a priority to develop your skills and those of your team.

Develop and Listen to Your Hiring "Gut"

- Classic business books like *Blink* by Malcolm Gladwell[4] and *Straight from the Gut* by Jack Welch reinforce the importance of developing your senses when it comes to making decisions. This skill can be developed—you need to learn to listen for the right information and listen to your own internal computer.
- Don't make hiring decisions out of consensus. The right person for you is the right person for you. In the end, you have to train, coach, and lead this individual, and you will be responsible for letting them go if you make a poor decision. So take responsibility for the decision. Take input from others as just that, input.

Overall, hiring people for their skills and experience, combined with our first step of properly scoping your job, will greatly reduce the risk of "falling in love with personality."

Create an Interview Process That Hires Stars

Hiring great people isn't just about moving quickly and having a straightforward interview process that focuses on the candidates' behaviors, strengths, and weaknesses. It's also about having a process that's effective. Most managers cringe when they hear the word "recruiting process." I cringe too because it reminds me of overly architected human resources processes that are not that efficient. What I'm going to give you is a few things to avoid in your process and a few things to do so that you can capitalize on the opportunity to recruit passive candidates.

Time Kills All Deals

You need to move on your interview process quickly. That means when you get a resume from a recruiter or you speak to someone who might be interested in having a conversation, you need to turn that conversation or resume around into an interview as quickly as possible. Long delays only allow the candidate's interest level to wane, things to change in their career, and the process to die. Move quickly and provide the candidate with a first class interview experience. If you have an administrative person scheduling interviews, make sure that person follows up, provides a cheery attitude, and says great things about the company.

The speed of your hiring process is extremely critical. To illustrate why, see the chart below. The concept of white heat is a widely accepted theory in the recruiting world.

The theory basically says that each time a company or a recruiter, or any individual interacts with the candidate, their interest level increases, while as time passes after that interaction, their interest level decreases.

Let's take an example. Our fictional candidate is sitting at his desk, not even thinking about looking for a job. He's had stellar reviews. He's performing in the top 10% of his company and he's an all-around good person with very, very high interpersonal skills. One day he receives a call from a recruiter. That recruiter provides him with compelling messaging about an opportunity that would allow him to learn, to grow, to work in an organization that is creating an impact on people's lives, and could lead to more career opportunities, ones aligned specifically with what he wants. It's not a vague outline but one that reveals specifics about what the opportunities are, why the company is growing, and how it will succeed.

Our fictional candidate is intrigued by the call. His level of interest increases above the baseline, high enough to consider looking at a new position. There's a line you have to cross in order to resign your job and go to another one, but he's taken the first step: he's interested in having an additional conversation.

Our fictional recruiter does a great job and secures some time with the candidate to discuss the opportunity in greater detail after work. The next day the recruiter and candidate speak again.

The candidate shares his career goals, aspirations, and some things that are happening in his current role that he believes may be standing in his way or impeding his ability to grow. As the candidate talks about his pain points and the future, and hears more from the recruiter about potential opportunities in the new company, his interest continues to grow, rising above the line of his previous conversation and reaching a new height. Immediately after the conversation with the recruiter ends, his interest level will start to decline. He'll start second guessing. A sales concept called buyer's remorse will weigh on him. He'll worry that it might be disloyal to leave his company. He'll wonder if he shouldn't just stick it out for a few more months, maybe another year until he'll gets that promotion. Maybe he'll get a new boss that will create more opportunities. Maybe he has a conversation with his spouse, a friend, about whether or not it's a good idea to leave. Self-doubt has crept in. "What if that company never calls back? What if they don't want to interview me? What if they don't like my background? I'm probably just fine in the job that I have. Maybe I should stick it out."

This doubting self-talk and the factor of time works on the candidate to slowly decrease his level of interest. It likely won't go back to where it was originally when he wasn't even interested, but give it enough time, it can. You want to keep your candidate above the next threshold, which is a desire to interview with the company. If you wait too long or don't respond, he might drop back down and not be interested in further conversation. When that happens, you've just lost a really good candidate. But let's assume you're moving quickly. If you move fast enough, you'll hit the candidate when he's still interested in having a phone interview with the manager.

If you schedule this quickly and don't allow too much time to elapse, he will remain engaged in the process and his interest level will continue to be high. Assuming you have an effective conversation between a hiring manager and a candidate on the telephone, you'll be able to assess the candidate's skills and fit, or traits and competencies, as well as, provide the ideal candidate with information that will attract that candidate. Assuming that conversation went well, we've now reached a third extremely high level of interest. The candidate has passed the gate of being interested in coming in for an interview. He or she might be willing to call in sick for work and get on an airplane, and fly across the country for an interview, or leave early, go to lunch, or claim a fake dentist appointment to come interview with you.

Regardless of the method used, the candidate has to have a significant level of interest to go through all that effort, especially since they're working and being well taken care of already. This is where recruiting is critical. It's important that we schedule and execute our face-to-face interview quickly, or the candidate once again may lose interest. Negative self talk may take over or others may intervene and talk the candidate out of going for an interview

Additionally, business circumstances can change. The candidate might receive a long awaited promotion, or complete a project that prompts kudos from his boss, or a senior leader may take him aside and engage him in a way that gets him very excited about their current organization. The result is you have now lost the high-performing candidate. The more time that elapses, the more possibility that this will happen. But if you continue to move quickly to the face-to-face interview, you preserve your golden opportunity.

Assuming the face-to-face interview goes well and you've identified this candidate as someone you want to hire, it's important to keep the candidate above what we call the point of white heat. This is the level at which the candidate is interested in making a job change. If their interest level falls below the point of white heat, they'll no longer be willing to go through with it, quit, and take a new job. This is why timing is so important. You need to continue to build on and enhance their interest level or it will decline. Time kills all deals and we must ensure a fast hiring process that provides a high level of salesmanship. And by salesmanship, I mean specific details about why the position is important, what the impact of this role will be, and what this could lead to for the right individual.

When you identify folks in your process that you're interested in, you and your organization need to spend the time educating the candidate on why they would want to do this job. Too often organizations' managers in interviews focus on screening out candidates and assessing their level of interest versus identifying candidates who have the skills and capabilities to be successful. Foster their interest by providing true life stories that help the candidate become excited about coming to work for the company. Hiring people is all about relationships. It's all about building trust, rapport, and friendship. People want to go to work for people in companies that they trust, they believe in, and they feel comfortable with. This all too human touch is often lost in bureaucratic, slow moving hiring processes that have been created by overzealous HR leaders, recruiters, and managers, who just don't understand the key secrets to hiring.

Create a fast, lean process that focuses on candidate attraction, not a heavily structured process that focuses on candidate screening. This is the key to identifying top performers. Never forget that top performers are happy. They're not looking. They're well-taken care of by their company. They have a long list of accomplishments. These accomplishments tell you about their past behaviors and past behaviors predict future performance.

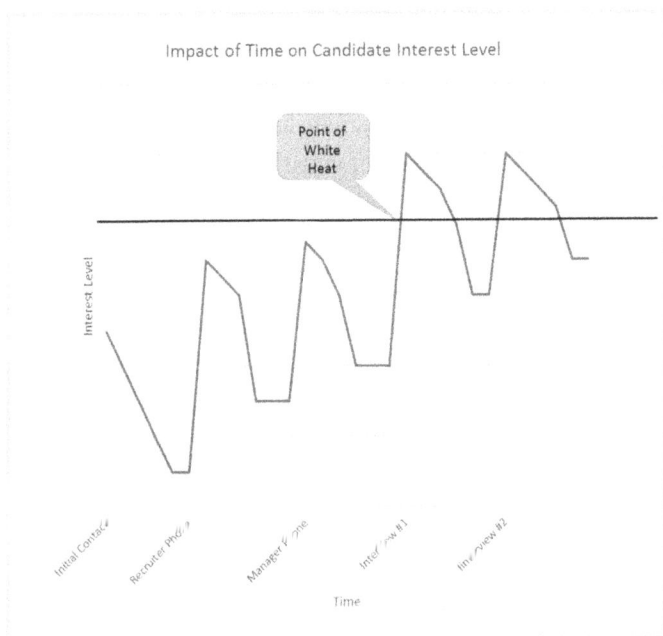

Impact of Time on Candidate Interest Level

Keep Your Interview Teams Small and Purposeful

Your interview shouldn't leave people exhausted. Some leaders in companies yield to the temptation to fit more people in for the interviews by doing panel interviews. At all cost, avoid panel interviews. They're highly ineffective. First, it's very difficult for the candidate to tailor his message to four, five, or six people at the same time. Second, it impedes the ability to create a bond between the candidate and the interviewer. This impacts the attractiveness of your organization, and quite frankly, can turn off top performers. And third, it doesn't allow any one individual to drill down deep enough on a candidate's background and experience, and instead creates a group mentality where others feel less than responsible for the hire and can lead to poor interviewing practices. So avoid those panel interviews.

Make Quick Decisions

Be sure to schedule or establish a debrief path immediately after the interview, or at minimum, within three days of the interview. This way if you're getting feedback from interviews, it's fresh, it's top of mind. It also means you can provide feedback to the candidates as quickly as possible. Again, when you understand the impact of the *white heat* model, you realize that it's imperative to move quickly through your process. Otherwise, you're going to lose the candidate.

Adapting to the Market and Making Great Hires

One of the most damaging mistakes that leaders make is to ignore the realities of the job market. Your goal in hiring is not to identify the "perfect" person who fits every bullet on your job description. The goal is to build a team that can accomplish the deliverables that you as a leader are responsible for delivering to your organization.

Sticking doggedly to a profile created without the reality of the market can leave a job open for way too long. There are three major items to consider.

Identify the Cost of Not Filling Your Job

Do some rough math. What is the estimated cost per month of not filling your opening? For a sales rep, this is easy to do. Let's say it's for a rep with a $5M annual quota. That's $100K in sales per week that you are not bringing in by not filling the job. Engineers can be more challenging, but give it a shot. If they are working on a $100M product that will launch next year, what is the cost of delay for each week or month that you are not filling the job?

Ensure that You Have Thoroughly Assessed the Market

In order to adapt to a market, you must have confidence that you understand it. Many managers wait for the ideal candidate to come across their desk without any knowledge of the market. Depending on your approach to identifying talent, you can either wait and hope or proactively map the market and methodically access the talent available.

Here at Med Device Talent, we identify between 100 to 150 individuals for each role we work on and methodically contact them. This process not only identifies the best candidates as quickly as possible, but also yields valuable market data useful in making a final decision. While results for individual roles vary, by using this process we typically identify three qualified candidates within the first 30 days.

You can gather this type of data from your HR team in order to understand who they have contacted and what the market looks like for your role. The faster you can understand the market and the more deeply you can penetrate the market, the faster you will fill your job with the best talent available.

Making a Decision

Now that you understand the cost of not filling your role and the market for the talent, you are in a position to trade off some of the "nice to have" Traits and Competencies for time. Meaning, the more urgent and costly it is to not have a position filled, the more you may have to compromise. The important point is that you realistically look at your current position and make decisions. Leaders who fail to hire, fail to adapt. They often live in fear of making a poor hire and never actually make the hire. Great employees can be developed since there is rarely the perfect candidate. It's your job to identify the right talent and keep moving forward.

CHAPTER 5:

Sell Your Job

One of the most important components of scoping out your role is identifying the What's In It For Me or WIFM of your position for potential candidates. As we've stated numerous times, the best candidates have multiple options. They're only going to accept your job if they feel it's the right career move for them. In order to attract these individuals, we need to become sales people for our positions.

If you're in sales, the tools to attract great candidates are right at your fingertips. For the rest of us, this is right about the point where we start to get uncomfortable. Selling, yuck, that's for salespeople right? Wrong, developing some basic sales skills is critical not only to attracting the right candidate to your job but generally in leading people. A significant component of visionary leadership is the ability to get people sold on your idea. Buckle up, I am about to help make you a stronger and more inspiring leader.

Selling 101

As you are probably aware, there are lots of bookstores and library bookshelves filled with sales books. As a development focused leader, it would be well worth your time to pick up one or two and invest in developing a deeper understanding of sales. Start with a copy of *How to Sell Anything to Anybody* by Joe Girard[5] and you will see that sales is all about relationships.

Here are three strategies you can implement today to bolster your ability to influence candidates:

- Focus on what's important to the other person you are selling to.
- Understand feature & benefits and focus on benefits.
- Appreciate the power of passion.

Focus on What's Important to the Person You're Selling to

The majority of what people hear when they are being sold anything is "blah, blah, blah, blah, blah." That is to say, they tune out and hear nothing. They only focus in and actually register the information you are providing when you speak about something that's actually important to them. In order to influence, you must be heard, and in order to be heard, you must be relevant.

There are two ways to provide more information that will be relevant. First, you can put yourself in the shoes of your ideal candidate and make some assumptions or educated guesses about what's important to him. This will allow you to construct messaging likely to resonate with him. This is what marketing and advertising people do, they write copy that is likely to connect with their reader. Much of the benefit of this book is to get inside the head of your ideal candidate so you can start thinking from his perspective and start developing messages that will excite him.

The second, more direct strategy is to ask probing

questions and then focus in on what they tell you is important. Questions like:

- How will you know you have found your next opportunity?
- What are you looking for in your next role (I don't mean money)?
- Describe your ideal next step.
- What do you like about your current role and what would you change?

You get the point, ask basic questions of your prospects and you will get information that you can use to sell them. Take that information and tell them about the things in your job that fit those needs.

Understanding Features & Benefits

A feature is a general characteristic of a product, service, or person. A benefit is what that product, service, or person can do for you. If you're still not tracking, take a moment to review the table below, and it should help you get a better feel for how this concept applies.

Feature	Benefits
Work on interesting products	You can gain experience that will make you more marketable
Great boss	Will help you develop and achieve your career goals
Growing company	You can grow your career

The concept is simple, take the description of what you're selling and translate it into how it impacts the person. Sales is about explaining the obvious so get over it and tell people why what you must sell is important to them.

In order to sell your role, you must be able to articulate the benefits of the role. For example, a feature of a new laundry detergent is ABC hexachloromine; it has a pleasant odor and it is less expensive. The benefit is that hexachloromine gets your clothes cleaner. The fresh scent makes the dirtiest of clothes smell nice and the price won't damage your pocketbook. Benefits are why people buy, so we need to talk about the benefits of our job.

First, start with the features of three key areas: your job, your management style, and your organization. What makes each area different, unique, or special? Remember, all tech companies are growing, all medical device companies are innovative, and all hospitals help people. These factors don't differentiate you. They make you sound like every other company. You need to find very specific, unique things about your organization, about your group, about your leadership, and about the job so that you can tell people what's special, compelling, or interesting about them.

By doing this, you'll have data, facts, and benefits that people can wrap their head around and become excited about. So, think about this and come up with your selling points. Number one, focus on the job. What will the job lead to? What is the impact of the job on your organization? What is the impact on your group and what is the impact for this individual? What type of visibility will this role have? Then, focus on what's exciting about working for you. What is it about your background, your management style, and how you develop people that will be interesting or exciting to a candidate?

Then consider the company? Be very specific. What is it about the culture that attracts you and gets you excited to come into work every day? What are the benefits of working at the organization? And I don't mean healthcare benefits and 401(k). I'm talking about what does it give you to work at the company. What does it feel like?

Create a worksheet to identify the features and benefits of your role now.

Feature & Benefit Worksheet

Describe the top 5 features of your Job Opening and turn them in to benefits.

Feature		Benefit
	→	

Feature		Benefit
	→	

Feature		Benefit
	→	

Feature

Benefit

Feature

Benefit

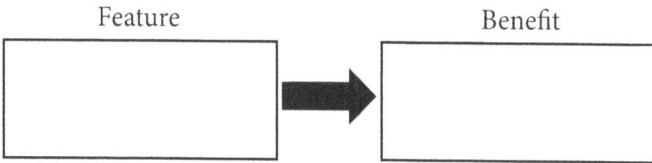

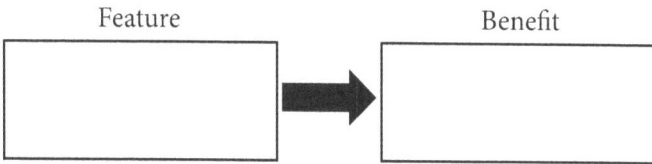

The Power of Passion

Sales is the transfer of emotion. Identify the feelings that you have about your role, about your organization, and be able to transfer those to the candidates. Excitement, opportunity, progress, impact – these are the type of things that we want to be able to share with candidates. Don't wait until a candidate asks: "What's so special about your company that I should consider coming to work here?"

Telling people about what gets you excited about your job, the company or the impact you can create is a powerful tool. Pay attention to the passionate excitement of anyone selling anything on television. If you don't believe your job is great, why would you expect anyone else to? Start telling your story with passion and people will connect more and be inspired.

Implementing the Three Sales Principles

Sales isn't that complicated. It's about investing time in understanding your customer, developing messaging, and delivering that message with passion. Too often, managers are too focused on their own needs and simply forget that the hiring process is like a marriage. You certainly would not expect a person to want to marry you just because you wanted a spouse. However, we expect people to want to come work for us just because there's a job opening. You need to invest time in the courting process, "taking long walks," and talking about a future together as a team. Selling great candidates is developing the relationship and focusing on what the other party is going to get out of the relationship.

Candidate Experience

Remember the old customer service adage, "One dissatisfied customer tells six people while one customer that's happy tells one." Well, the same is true for an exciting and interesting interview experience. If you give someone a great interview experience, even if it's not exactly the right role but you give them good feedback, they are actually going to share that experience with someone. They'll admire your company and maybe apply in the future.

If you give them a poor experience, they'll tell six people and other people won't apply for your role. This is the problem with the shotgun approach to recruitment. You simply interview too many people and never hire them. By targeting the individuals that you reach out to, attract, interview, and ultimately hire, you're able to provide a quality experience for each individual.

This is another reason why interviewing more candidates is not better. More candidates take up resources. At the end of the day, there is a significant amount of labor hours that go into candidates that we don't hire. Perhaps it's 10 minutes to review a resume, 30 minutes for a phone screen, then it's a face-to-face interview with four people for an hour each. That's four labor hours. Plus a debrief with the whole team, another labor hour. Before you're done, you're up to five or six hours per candidate. All that time is wasted when a candidate isn't hired. So identifying the right candidates to attract into your process can save quite a bit of resources, help result in a better brand for your organization, and ultimately increase your probability of a good hire.

In my business, I focus on sending three qualified candidates for each role. I don't send more than that. Sometimes I only send one but my aim is always to provide high quality candidates that fit the role and are capable of doing it. Because if I'm able to do that, then the company is left choosing between one, two, or three people that can do the job instead of trying to determine who's capable of doing the job and not having the time to determine who's a top performer. If you have to pick from several people that can do the job, then you can focus on identifying the top performer.

Create a Hiring Process That Consistently Exceeds Expectations

I had an utterly mediocre boss once who would constantly compare our company to other companies. He would say, "If you think it's bad here, take a look at XYZ they are worse." No wonder that person isn't going anywhere with his career. Comparing yourself to mediocrity is setting the bar low. You need to strive to achieve an experience that sets you apart in a good way.

Speed

I have seen more than one candidate "swept off their feet" by a company that had the ability to move quickly. A thorough yet expedient hiring process communicates a sense of inevitability to a candidate and can get him to say yes. He feels like it was meant to be. Long processes prompt candidates to "second guess," and worse, allows time for your competitors or their own company to swoop in and steal them away.

Make People Feel Important

Give the candidate a great interview experience. If an admin is making the arrangements, make sure they appreciate how important it is to move quickly, communicate, and give the candidate a great first impression of your company.

If they're relocating, give the candidate a great travel experience so that they'll think the most of your location and organization. Arranging for the person stay near a scenic location like a beach, park, or other attraction can help sell your area much better than putting someone near an airport or unattractive location. In preparing for the interview, you should meet face to face, if possible, or on the phone with your interview team. Your interview team should consist of no more than five individuals with various backgrounds who are capable of both assessing the candidate and selling the opportunity. Even though you might be schooled in an attractive interview process that's exciting to candidates, if you put in an interrogator, you could blow the whole deal.

Attracting Great Candidates Means Selling Yourself

Ultimately, people leave managers whom they do not believe in and they go work for leaders whom they do believe in. That means that selling your job and your company involves selling yourself. Most of us aren't sales people. If you are, you're probably very good at this. If you're not, you need some advice here.

It's critically important to understand what's important to the people you're speaking to. So how do you do this? Well, first, you can ask good questions like, "What's important to you?" or "What are you looking for in your next opportunity?" or "How will you know you found the right job, the right person to work for?"

When people start to tell you what's important to them, you really get a view into their values. We've all had the experience of hiring a person whom we thought was great, only to have the person that actually shows up on the start date be highly demanding or significantly under-skilled. If you ask people what's important to them and listen to their answers, they will get comfortable and start to reveal those types of things. Ask good follow-up questions like, "Hey, you mentioned that pay is important to you. How do you know you're being paid right? What makes you feel like it's the most important thing?"

If they're extremely focused on compensation and are undercompensated in their current role, you might ask why or you might think about why and try to find the reason. Being underpaid is typically a red flag and a signal that something might be wrong here. While there are some really good people who are underpaid, and those candidates create a good market opportunity, it's far more frequent that underpaid individuals have some sort of performance issue that you need to identify.

Making the Match

Making the match is about aligning values and goals between the manager and the candidate. In order to do this, you need to understand the goals and values of the candidate, and you need to take some time to think about yours. You should be able to articulate your goals as a leader, your values, and what you're trying to drive in your organization. This will be attractive to the right people and may turn off the wrong people. But that's fine. Being who you are is really important.

I once spent some time with a psychologist when I was going through my divorce. He said his business was all about dealing with zebras who thought they were lions and lions who thought they were zebras. He said if people would just accept who they are and what they are, they'd be a lot happier and a lot more effective. So if you're a lion, be a lion, and if you're a zebra, be a zebra.

This is very true for a leader who wants to attract potential followers. You need to be true to who you are, just as candidates need to be true to who they are in the interview process. Otherwise, you get a poor match because the person you thought you were hiring or the company the candidate thought he was going to work for is false. So be true to yourself and spend some time understanding who you are as a leader, why people would want to work for you, and how to discuss this with other people. This isn't rocket science. Hiring people is all about interfacing with people. Get good at talking to people, creating relationships, and getting past all the corporate jargon.

This isn't a bunch of sales bull. If you relate at a basic level, person to person, not manager to candidate, interviewer to applicant, but person to person on an equal playing field, you'll get to know this person in a way that you can't in a formal interview setting. And if your beliefs and values align with this individual's beliefs and values, you will have made a match that is highly effective.

Beware of the tendency to overcomplicate what is essentially a simple process. Avoid elaborate sourcing strategies, excessive data, highly-structured interviews, and assessments that only serve to clutter up the communication. Keep it simple. Hiring great people is about finding out what matters to them, forming a relationship, and building a bond. If you can do this, you will hire amazing people.

Make Great Offers

While this book isn't a tutorial on offer negotiation, I do want to give you some insight into what it takes to attract top performers. When you create your profile, it's important to understand that individuals you want to attract aren't looking to make a lateral move, in spite of your strong sales process and exciting opportunity. Top performers have been trained to expect top increases. If you look at any organization in the United States, their top performers are the best paid people. They're typically given raises in excess of 3% to 5% a year and promotions every 18 to 24 months. If you think you're going to be able to give a top performing person who is not even looking for a job a lateral move or a pay decrease, the odds aren't in your favor.

The trick here is to hire at the right level. If you look to hire somebody who is extremely experienced and maxes out your budget, you're going to be in deep trouble. If you have deep pockets and you're able to hire for their experience and give them a premium, then absolutely go for it. But if you have a budget constraint, consider hiring at a little bit lower level and include more performance capabilities. You'll get a top performing person with high potential, a lot of capability, and they'll fit your budget. Whatever you do, don't go down the road and waste your time on people you can't hire. The worst thing that can happen to you is a rejected offer.

Rejected offers do happen even under the best circumstances but there's some things you can do to avoid them. Number one, ensure that your compensation is aligned with the current compensation and expectations of the candidate that you're recruiting. Assume that you're going to need to provide a premium for them to come to your company. If you're on a tight budget, a conversation early on about their expectations might make sense. But keep in mind, people's expectations vary throughout the process. The more interested someone is in a position, typically, the lower their expectations. Meaning, a candidate may be willing to accept a little less compensation if they feel like the position is exciting, provides a great career opportunity, or will do something to get them where they want to go.

Conversely, if your position offers little growth and no exciting opportunities, the premium that you'll need to pay is much higher, as top-performing candidates are smart enough to know that there might not be as much growth. They may still be willing to take the opportunity but they're going to expect a higher premium. So be clear about the relationship between opportunity and compensation. When making an offer, I highly suggest that you don't get into a negotiation or a niggling situation. It's always best to come out with your best offer first. I know this is highly controversial since individuals enjoy negotiating and believe that it's an important component to the process.

If you feel like a candidate needs to have a negotiation, then perhaps leave something in the bank. But otherwise, it's better to explain that you are focused on making the best offer first and this is what you believe is the best thing that the organization can do for the individual. Don't try to get cheap here and save a couple of bucks. If your game is to attract radically successful talent, you're going to have to take radically successful measures to acquire that talent. And that means good offers, not skimpy offers.

CHAPTER 6:

Putting It All Together

The four secrets of recruiting work together as a system to attract the right people to you and your organization. It's not that complicated:

1. Identify the skills, experience and attributes you need.
2. Develop and implement a strategy to approach and attract top performers.
3. Create an interview process that assesses and attracts.
4. Finally, sell your job by focusing on benefits and creating a relationship with your candidate.

The hard part is actually sticking to the plan and avoiding the trap of allowing the team's focus to drift from targeted attraction to "sourcing." Implementing this solution takes discipline and execution. However, the results can be radical. This is the secret ingredient to the success of Edwards Lifesciences. When I joined the company, it was an unknown spin-off of Baxter Healthcare with $800 million in sales and 5,000 employees. When I walked out the door, the company had over $2.7 billion in sales and 10,000 employees. The stock had increased from thirteen dollars to two hundred and sixty dollars a share. I recently had a chat with the retired head of HR for Edwards, Rob Reindel. Rob credits much of the Edwards success to the quality of talent we were able to acquire. The secret to the quality of talent was implementing the advice I've outlined in this book.

A question that may come up: How do I apply this strategy for roles where it's impossible to hire from a competitor? Examples of this are new graduate or entry level positions and roles that are brand new to a market.

Hiring Entry Level Positions

Applying the Radical Hiring success philosophy to entry level hiring is relatively simple. As you consider the planning phase of this type of hire, it's important to recognize that most new graduates are hired for traits and less for competencies. That is to say that, at this level we hire for potential and personality more than experience. Therefore, our planning must be appropriately rigorous around the character traits that are most critical to success. Don't totally ignore competencies, but you will have less to go on here.

In the attraction phase, applicants don't provide a significantly poorer pool of candidates. Referrals are still very important, but a well written job description just might yield some great candidates.

In the interview phase you likely will need to focus more on assessment than on experienced candidates as there will be more people to choose from. You can still use behavior interviewing to investigate the traits and competencies of candidates, but be sure to look for stories that support the drive, motivation, and skills that you seek. These stories may be more in life experience than in work examples. Look back at yourself, can you see examples of the man or woman you would become in business in your high school and college work? If I look back at the Mike Adamo coming out of graduate school, the same spirit of independence, innovation, drive, and lack of detail orientation were visible and easy for someone who was looking to find these traits.

Bring It All Together: The Cost of Declined Offers

In this book, you've learned how to identify, attract, and ultimately hire top performing individuals. I'd be remiss not to invest a few minutes talking about the cost of not hiring these individuals. What I mean by this is the cost of extending offers that aren't accepted. This is literally the worst sin in recruitment. By the time you get to the offer stage, you've invested enormous time and energy to find top performing individuals. You've interviewed them, assessed their fit and their experience. And finally, you've made them an offer. Think about the hours that have gone into each step of this process.

When an offer is rejected, you're back to square one. You've likely passed on pursuing other candidates to focus on this individual. "Oh, well…things happen." This is not the approach you want to take. Offer declines are almost 100% preventable, but it's up to you as the leader to drive a recruitment process that avoids them. If it took three months to get to this point, it may take you another three months to repeat it. That's six months to hire. So here's how to prevent offer declines.

First, focus on people who are happy and not looking. A high percentage of declined offers come from candidates who accept other jobs. That means they have to be interviewing for other jobs and looking at multiple opportunities to decline your offer. By focusing on high achievers who are engaged in their jobs, you avoid wasting time with active job seekers who ultimately may or may not choose you.

Second, sell your job. The more attracted a candidate is to your position, the opportunity, and you, the less likely he is to decline your offer. If you've created a relationship with this person through the interview process by building rapport, by getting to know each other, and by creating aligned values and vision, it's unlikely he will decline your offer.

Third, make good offers. You can lowball poor performing people. You can lowball people who are active job seekers. But lowballing high performing individuals is a mistake you will pay for. Your compensation should be in line with the expectations of high performing individuals and your offer needs to reflect that.

By bringing together these three components: focusing on happy, engaged individuals who are high performing, creating a sales process that's highly effective, and making offers that are aggressive and fair, you will significantly reduce the number of offer declines and increase the likelihood of hiring a high-performing individual. After all, many of the declines you get are from the highest performing individuals because they have choices.

In Conclusion, Apply the Great Truths of Recruitment and You Will Achieve Radical Hiring Success:

- **Top performers for your job are doing a similar job at a competitor.** Find them and convince them to quit and work for you. That's what recruiting is!
- **Candidates leave bad bosses to go to good bosses.** Become the most attractive boss you can be.
- **Top performers leave clues.** Look and listen for these clues.
- **Eagles Fly with Eagles and Turkeys flock with Turkeys.** Build a network of top performers.
- **Time Kills all Deals.** Faster interview processes are better.

Notes

1. Welch, Jack, and John A. Byrne. *Jack: Straight from the Gut*. Warner Business Books, 2001.
2. Lombardo, Michael M., and Robert W. Eichinger. *FYI: For Your Improvement: A Guide for Development and Coaching*. Minneapolis, MN: Lominger International, 2009. Print.
3. Reindl, Rob, and Mike Mussallem. *The HOW of Leadership: Unleashing the Capacity of Your People*. Visual Insights Press, 2014 Print.
4. Gladwell, Malcolm. *Blink: The Power of Thinking without Thinking*. New York : Little, Brown and Co., 2005.
5. Girard, Joe. *How to Sell Anything to Anybody*. New York: Fireside, , 2006.

About the Author

Mike Adamo is the author of *This Book Will Get You Hired for The Job You Want* and founder of Med Device Talent. With almost twenty years' experience in medical device recruitment, including leading corporate talent acquisition and third party executive search, Mike is one of the industry's leading talent acquisition experts. Mike's mission is to help organizations and individuals grow by aligning talented individuals with exceptional opportunities. Med Device Talent is a full-service talent acquisition provider to the medical device industry.

Prior to founding Med Device Talent, Adamo was the recruiting leader for Edwards Lifesciences for over 10 years. He was the top recruiting expert, leading the company's growth from 5,000 to 10,000 employees. During his tenure, he led the recruitment of over 100 of the company's top executives, including corporate vice presidents, board members, and operating leaders.

Adamo led major hiring scaleups in Singapore, China, and the US. He consulted on projects in Europe, Latin America, and the Caribbean. Adamo was at the recruiting helm as the company scaled up R&D, Regulatory, Clinical, Marketing, and Sales to launch the world's first Trans Cather Heart Valve.